The Flock And Their Shepherds: An Attempt To Describe The Members, Pastors, Ordinances And Mission Of The Church Of God

Partridge And Oakey Publisher

In the interest of creating a more extensive selection of rare historical book reprints, we have chosen to reproduce this title even though it may possibly have occasional imperfections such as missing and blurred pages, missing text, poor pictures, markings, dark backgrounds and other reproduction issues beyond our control. Because this work is culturally important, we have made it available as a part of our commitment to protecting, preserving and promoting the world's literature. Thank you for your understanding.

THE

FLOCK AND THEIR SHEPHERDS.

AN ATTEMPT TO DESCRIBE THE

MEMBERS, PASTORS, ORDINANCES, AND MISSION

OF THE

CHURCH OF GOD.

DEDICATED TO ALL WHO

LOVE ZION, AND LOVE PEACE.

LONDON:
ARTRIDGE AND OAKEY, PATERNOSTER ROW;
AND 14, BUCHANAN STREET, GLASGOW;
(JOHN M'COMBE, AGENT.)

MDCCCXLVII.

THE
FLOCK AND THEIR SHEPHERDS,
ETC. ETC.

"THE CHURCH OF GOD WHICH HE HATH PURCHASED WITH HIS OWN BLOOD."

THE term Church simply means an assembly, be the object of that assembly what it may; thus, in the very last verse of the chapter preceding that in which the word receives the sacred application, "the church of God which he hath purchased with his own blood," it is used of the persecuting crowd at Ephesus, which the town clerk rebuked for its tumult, and "dismissed the assembly," or church. In the New Testament the word, as employed in a religious sense, has two distinct applications; first, to the whole number of God's people, "Christ also loved the church, and gave himself for it;" secondly, to the believers of any given locality, or assembling in any particular place; "Nymphas and the church which is in his house," "the church o Ephesus." No case occurs in Scripture in which the word is used in the sense now so familiar, of a building for the purpose of worship. Originally designating the assembly, it has come, by a very natural transfer, to designate the building where the assembly takes place; but this, though a very allowable, is not a scriptural use of the term.

No definition of a church can be more simple, more scriptural, or more exact, than that given by the Church of England, namely, "A congregation of faithful men, where the true word of God is preached, and the sacraments duly administered." This is an individual church, and the whole church is but the individual churches taken collectively.

It will be necessary to consider the church as to her MEMBERS, her PASTORS, her ORDINANCES, and her MISSION.

I. THE MEMBERS OF THE CHURCH.

The first point requiring notice under this head is the *condition of membership*. The church is not a promiscuous crowd of men, assembled without any regard to character or belief, a crowd in which Jew and Infidel, Mohammedan and Christian, might meet. Its very nature supposes some conditions, by which a common character will be given to all its members. It is important to know what those conditions, as laid down in Scripture, are, lest we should, on the one hand, reject from the church those whom the Saviour receives; or, on the other, receive into the church those who reject the Saviour.

If our Lord have taught us the condition on which He receives men, then it will scarcely be doubted that we have the condition on which the CHURCH ought to receive them. "Him that cometh to me I will in no wise cast out," said the Redeemer, (John vi. 37,) and presently added, " No man can come to me except the Father which hath sent me draw him." Christ then receives all who, being drawn of the Father, come to Him, and the church ought to receive all who, being drawn of the Father, are coming to Christ. The only question that rests for the Church is, what evidence ought to be held as satisfactorily proving that persons belong to this class? For an answer we must look to the conduct of our Lord's apostles.

As baptism was the sign of admission into the Church, the condition required by the apostles for baptism was of course their condition of church membership. Now the first discourse preached under the new dispensation, was addressed to men utterly ignorant of the Gospel scheme, and inimical to its author. Yet when the truth proclaimed has so been applied to their hearts, that they cry, "What must we do?" the apostle at once replies, "Repent and be baptized." Here the only condition named, in order to admission to the Church, is repentance, and of its reality no other evidence could be given than the declaration and demeanour of the applicants. Again, when the eunuch makes a direct application for admission to the church, by demanding, "What hindereth that I should be baptized?" Philip rejoins, "If thou believest with all thine heart thou mayest." Here the only condition named is faith, and the only evidence of the character of that faith is the eunuch's own declaration, "I believe that Jesus Christ is the Son of God," a declaration which certainly proved no more than that, being drawn of the Father, he was sincerely coming to Christ. Again, when Peter had received the Gentiles into the church, and found it necessary to vindicate the step, he did so simply by alleging the fact that they had received the Holy Ghost.

Now in each of these cases the persons applying for admission were ignorant of all questions of ecclesiastical discipline, and of all doctrinal detail. On such matters they were not interrogated, nor was a delay in order to instruct them judged necessary; the eye of the church looked just to the same point, as the eye of her Head. Were these men drawn of the Father, and coming to the Son? Their avowed belief in Christ's divine character and saving office, and their earnestness, attested that they were so, and no more was required. The like belief, accompanied by the like earnestness, are the only evidence we can have that men are coming to Christ. Having these they have the scriptural condition of membership, and no other ought to be sought; no man has any right to demand another.

The next point demanding attention is the *sign of membership*. Baptism is the sign of admission into the church; but having received that sacrament is not in itself a sign of actual membership, for a person once baptized may apostatise even so far as to " count the blood of the covenant wherewith he was sanctified an unholy thing." As baptism is the sign of admission, so the other sacrament, the Lord's supper, is the sign of actual union with the Church; to admit an individual to that holy table is to recognise him as in the church; to exclude him is to deny his membership, and that not his membership in any particular denomination, but in the church of Christ at all. For no community celebrates the Saviour's death as Episcopalians, or Baptists, or Presbyterians, or Methodists; but all as followers of Jesus Christ. In that character alone do they approach the Lord's table, and to deny the fellowship of that table to any one, is not to deny his episcopacy, or his congregationalism, but to deny him a place among Christ's people. Such an exclusion is a grave step, but one which, in proper cases, must be firmly taken. The rule for such cases is stated with perfect clearness in God's holy word, "Now we command you, brethren, in the name of the Lord Jesus, that ye withdraw yourselves from every brother that walketh disorderly" (2 Thess. iii. 6). Again, some arose who "confessed not that Jesus Christ is come in the flesh," and regarding such an one we are directed—" receive him not into your house, neither bid him God speed." Here then are two grounds on which we are not only safe in denying the real Christianity of a professing Christian, but strictly required to do so, by our Master's authority. A denial of our Lord's incarnation and atonement, or a rebellion against his lawful reign—refusing in doctrine the person of Christ, or refusing in life his command, form the only cases in which we have a Scripture warrant for rejecting the fellowship of a professed believer. We have no other rule given; on the region of the heart man's eye intrudes not, God has reserved that for his own inspection; but in doing so He has made it our duty to mark the fruits, and to "know" men accordingly. Every church ought to possess and to exercise the right of denying a place at the Lord's table to all who walk disorderly, and to all who deny the Lord that bought them. But if a member of Christ's church ask me for admission to that table, I dare not stipulate that he shall leave his own communion and join mine, that he shall dismiss his own convictions and receive mine. To propose such terms to one who avows faith in the Redeemer, is to change that table from being the Lord's table, and to make it my table:— to require that concurrence with me shall be joined to faith in Christ, and to assume the awful province of denying, on grounds for which I have no warrant, the memorials of the Saviour's death, to one who avers his hope in the Saviour's blood. I dare not do it.

We next consider the *Duties of Membership*. The first duty of a member of the church is to love the brotherhood; "by this we know that we are passed from death unto life, because we love the brethren." This love must not be grounded on any natural quality, any mental characteristics, or any sympathy of views with our own; these may be perfectly legitimate grounds for such an intimate companionship as can subsist only with a few; but for the *love* which is the due of all, no other basis may be owned, no other plea required, than that they pertain to Jesus. I must love them, not because, like me, they are "of Paul" or "of Apollos," not because they "regard the day," or "eat only herbs," or "eat all things," following just the same views as myself; but because, whether they regard the day or not, whether they eat the meat or not, it is done or not done "unto the Lord." Once aware that my brother is "fully persuaded in his own mind," that Episcopacy, or Presbyterianism, or any other form of church order, is according to the will of God, then let me honour and love him for maintaining that which he believes to be pleasing to my Lord. His judgment or my judgment errs; but if he upholds only that which he believes to be after the mind of the Spirit, and if I uphold only that which I believe to be after the mind of the Spirit, then his heart is as my heart, and we are intimately one;

our affections are upon the same centre, and our aim towards the same point. Let me not then despise my brother, even though he seem to me "weak in the faith;" let me receive him, and that "not to doubtful disputations," but to open arms and warm affections. Let me by no means chill him to a distance, "for God hath received him." This is an answer to all my zeal for a creed without a flaw, and a ritual without a redundancy. "God hath received him", and he loves truth;—"God hath received him," and he loves order;— "God hath received him," and he loves love, but hatred he hateth sorely;—"God hath received him." It is enough; Come to my arms, my brother. "We are members one of another," "he that is joined to the Lord is one spirit;" we are closer than all the art of earth could twine us. In the sweets of this union, let us dwell and rejoice, till death undo all possibility of parting.

The most grievous offence against brotherly love is to "cause divisions" in the body of Christ; those who do so we are required to "mark" and to "avoid." It is desirable clearly to understand what causing divisions is. The Christian who goes out into the unconverted world and turning a wanderer thence leads him into any flock of Christ's people, cannot be accused of dividing the fold. He is increasing the fold of Christ, and dividing that of the adversary. We bid him God speed. On the other hand we cannot acquit a person of "causing divisions" merely because he declares that his object is not to divide but to unite. In so saying he may be perfectly sincere, his heart may be full of a project of unity; but let him ask, In what is this unity to consist? Is it not in this, that all shall embrace his views on the topics which excite him, and enter into the opinions which he deems so harmonious and beautiful? Can the grand scheme of unity with which his heart is big ever be effected in any other way? And if not, he will at once perceive that this object—universal conformity to himself, is precisely the one set before him by every "disputer of this world." Men do not force forward their dogmas in order to have them rejected, but to have them embraced; and the highest aim of their ambition would be to see all conquered by their argument, and converts to their views. No sooner does a man allow his zeal for universal concurrence in his own opinions, to lead him to push those opinions disputatiously upon his brethren, than he begins to cause divisions, and the more he urges his purpose of unity, the more he divides. His wish, it is true, is for unity; but he may be assured that if his desire for unity lead him to write, to circulate, or to engender "disputations" designed to prove that no good man ought to belong to the Church of England, or the Church of Scotland, or the Dissenters, or any other branch of Christ's Church than that with which he is himself connected; then his labours directly tend to increase the divisions of God's people, and have no other tendency whatsoever. If he lead sinful men to a knowledge of the Saviour, he increases the number of those who are one in Him; if he lead Christ's people to a fuller conformity to his image, he increases the sense and the manifestation of their union. The true path of union lies in the attempt to convert sinners, and to conform saints to Christ. But the attempt to make every Christian think as I do, upon points of Church usage, is a search after uniformity; and, like all searches after uniformity that have been made from the beginning, will issue only in division. Divisions do not result from difference of opinion, but from the desire to make others surrender to our arguments on the points wherein we differ.

It is of principles as of men, "by their fruits ye shall know them;" accordingly Saint Paul traces this divisive spirit to a carnal state of mind. "For whereas there is among you envying, and strife, and divisions, are ye not carnal and walk as men?" (1 Cor. iii. 3.) Your desire to make others " see as you do," begets strife, and strife begets division. Now the feeling which bears such fruit can only be carnal. The individual, or the community addicted to the intrusion of their own peculiarities on their *Christian Brethren* with a view to disputation or proselyting, are so far, and lamentably, carnal. They may judge very differently of their own state of heart; but the Apostle has decided their case; they are only "babes in Christ," lacking as yet large growth in holy love. Those who are spiritual, who have learned that the " servant of the Lord should not strive" (with the friends of his Lord, though with his enemies contend earnestly he must,)—they, are bound to bear the infirmity of these weaker brethren, and to overcome their fault by love.

Next to the duty of mutual love is that of *mutual edification*. The relation of believers to the Lord is beautifully represented by that of the branch to the vine; namely, complete and unchangeable dependance. But this emblem does not set forth the relation of the believer both to his Lord and to his brethren; for that the only suitable figure is the body, in which every member while depending primarily on the head, has a dependancy also on every other member, not one of which exists merely for its own development, but each has an office for the common benefit. The Apostle says, (Eph. iv. 16,) "In whom the whole body, fitly joined together, and compacted by that which *every joint* supplieth, according to the effectual working in the measure of *every part*, maketh increase of the body to the edifying of itself in love." Again, (Col. ii. 19,) "The head from which the whole body by joints and bands having nourishment ministered, increaseth with the increase of God." These passages alone sufficiently demonstrate that the strength and growth of the whole body (the Church) depends in part on each member, and that he who does not in his measure aid toward its "making increase" and "edifying itself," fails of his appointed duty. Too many Christians look upon themselves as called only to receive grace, but never in any way to convey it. This, however, is not the calling of any one of God's children; they have every one a part to bear in the action of their Lord's body, and as the smallest joint or the obscurest muscle moves for the benefit of the entire frame, so must each believer contribute by his own life toward the faith, the strength, and the increase of the whole church.

This mutual edification may be promoted by STIMULATING EXAMPLE, "consider one another to provoke to love and to good works (Heb. x. 24); by SPIRITUAL CONVERSATION, "they that feared the Lord spake often one to another, and the Lord hearkened and heard it, and a book of remembrance was written before him for them that feared the Lord and thought upon his name" (Mal. iii. 16); by mutual ADMONITION, CONFESSION, and PRAYER; "teaching and admonishing one another" (Col. iii. 16); "Exhorting one another," (Heb. x. 25); "Confess your faults one to another, and pray one for another," (Jas. v. 16). These duties are essential to a healthy state of a church, and cannot be wholly omitted without utter inaction and disease. In some branches of the church, mutual edification is left depending on the zeal of the members in their occasional and undirected intercourse; in others regular provision is made to promote it, by meetings for reading the Scriptures, or by prayer meetings, or class meetings. But whether a Christian belongs to a branch of the church which has such regular provision or not, the duty lies equally upon him to aid, by word and deed, the edification of his brethren.

Another duty of membership is, *sympathy with the brethren, and support of those who are poor*. This duty, as indeed the one last named, is included in the great duty of love; for, where we "love in truth," we will rejoice with those that do rejoice, and weep with those that weep. If our brother be in sorrow, he must have our sympathy; if in indigence, our goods. A kindly tear will assuage his grief, but will not supply his want; for that he must have, not a tear, but a gift. "Whoso hath this world's good, and seeth his brother have need, and shutteth up his bowels of compassion from him, how dwelleth the love of God in him?" He who does not give of his own goods for the relief of needy brethren, is a most unfaithful member of the church.

II. We now come to consider the PASTORS OF THE CHURCH. In the New Testament, two classes of officers are named: the one for the temporal affairs of the church—deacons; (Acts vi. 2—6.); the other, "for the edifying of the body of Christ." This latter class included (Eph. iv. 11) "Apostles," those who were witnesses of our Lord's resurrection.* "Prophets," who, by special gift, foretold things to come. "Evangelists," who

* In 1 Cor. xv. 7, 8, 9, Paul evidently connects his being an apostle with the fact that he had seen the *Lord risen*. See also, Acts i. 29.

went abroad into the world to gather a flock where none existed before. "Pastors and teachers," who watched over flocks already formed, and fed them with the truth.

The words, "Feed the church of God, which he hath purchased with his own blood," were, we are told (ver. 17), addressed to the "elders of the church." These same elders are called "bishops;" "Take heed to yourselves, and to the flock over which the Holy Ghost hath made you overseers," that is, bishops; for St. Paul used the very same word here, as when he said, "If any man desire the office of a bishop, he desireth a good work." These same individuals, therefore, were elders and bishops; it is not necessary here to prove more largely, that the two terms designated the same order of ministers.†

† It is worthy of remark, that in the two passages, (1 Cor. xii. 28; Eph. iv. 11) which enumerate the orders of the ministry, ordinary and extraordinary, no mention is made either of bishops or elders. They must then be included in some of the orders named. They cannot be included under apostles, for the persons addressed (Acts xx. 28) were bishops, but they certainly were not apostles. None

It is necessary to consider the SEPARATE-
NESS of the pastoral office. Some Christians
raise a doubt, as to whether any distinctions
exist among believers, holding that under
the Christian dispensation no priestly order
is recognised, but that all God's people are
equally " kings and priests;" "a royal priesthood;" and inferring, that because all are
equally priests, therefore all have the same
spiritual office to fulfil. Nothing can be
plainer than that, in the New Testament,
no believer is a " priest," in any sense above
that in which every believer is a " priest."
Not a passage is to be found, where the
term " priest " is applied to any minister
of the Gospel, or, indeed, to any *individual
Christian* at all. In Christianity there is
no priest but the Lord Jesus, and no sacrifice

will contend that they were included under prophets
or evangelists. It then remains only that they
were included under " pastors and teachers " in the
one case, and " teachers " in the other. A church
is a flock, the minister is its pastor—that is, shep-
herd; a church is a school, the minister is its
teacher; a church is a family, the minister is its
elder; the church is a temple in progress, the
minister is its overseer or bishop.

but he; it is, therefore, impossible there should be a priestly order, nor is such an order ever hinted at in the apostolic writings. Christ on high is the one Priest of the church; she has none on earth; and so completely is this the case, that it is said of our Lord himself, (Heb. viii. 4,) that "If he were on earth, he should not be a priest." Those who contend for the "open priesthood," stand on ground purely scriptural, and, therefore, impregnable. No Scripture shows one Christian to be a priest, except as every Christian is so.

But the inference drawn from this fact is, that because there is no priest, therefore there is no pastor, or that, because the priesthood is exercised by all, therefore the pastorate is exercised by all. Now, is this conclusion scriptural? Is it true that "every Christian is a minister?" St. Paul says, (1 Cor. xii. 28, 29,) "For God hath set *some* in the church, first apostles, secondarily prophets, thirdly teachers, &c. . . . . Are all apostles? Are all prophets? Are all teachers?" And again, (Eph. iv. 11,) " He gave *some* apostles, and *some* prophets, and *some* pastors and teachers, for the perfecting of the saints." Surely this does not mean that all the saints were thus set in the church; but that some were so set for the perfecting of all. "We beseech you to know them which labour among you, and are *over you* in the Lord, and admonish you." (1 Thess. v. 12.) Here is a manifest pre-eminence given to some above others. "Remember them which have the rule over you, who have spoken unto you the Word of God." (Heb. xiii. 17.) And in ver. 17 of the same chapter, "Obey them that have the rule over you, and submit yourselves, for they watch for your souls, as they that must give account." It is fully as impossible to believe that these counsels were addressed to churches where all were equal in office, as it is to believe that all the family are to be "elders," all the school "teachers," all the builders "overseers," or all the flock "shepherds." Our Lord, in "going up on high" to intercede for his church, did not give her on earth any priests, for she needed no more sacrifice for sins; but he did give her "some pastors," for the perfecting of the saints, for the work of the ministry, for the edifying of the body of Christ.

"It is also necessary to enquire, whether the separateness of the pastoral office demands *a withdrawal from secular engagements, and an exclusive consecration to the work of the ministry*. The New Testament does not teach the affirmative of this question in any way which would exclude from active spiritual duties all, except those who are "separated to the Gospel." On the contrary, it is plain that some who were not so separated fulfilled useful offices for the spread and increase of piety. Nor is it possible to prove that preaching was confined to the pastorate, but most probable that no one became a pastor, until, as a preacher, he had proved himself "apt to teach." Few churches exist, which do not, more or less, recognise the eligibility of laymen for spiritual duties, by employing them as catechists, licentiates, local preachers, or under some other designation, to labour for the awakening of sinners, and the edification of saints. The exclusion of the laity from all spiritual functions, as it is manifestly without sanction in the work of God, so also is it attended with great danger, leading the people to feel as if the work of God pertained, in no sense to them, and favouring the most unscriptural sentiment, that the clergy are the church.*

But this does not at all embarrass the question, as to whether the pastor is only a member of the church, exercising spiritual functions, but still engaged in worldly affairs; or is set apart wholly to feed the flock of God. That the latter is the case, appears proved, as plainly as possibly could be, by the fact that the flock are required to support the pastor. "Let him that is taught in the Word, communicate to him that teacheth in all good things." (Gal. vi. 6.) This, certainly, would not be necessary, if he were supporting himself by a worldly calling. But the matter is placed beyond dispute, and beyond appeal, by 1 Cor. ix. 14, "Even so hath the Lord

* The subject of lay agency is well treated in a recent work, entitled, "Perilous Times," by G. Smith, F.A.S., &c. &c.

c

ordained, that they who preach the Gospel should live of the Gospel." The separation of the ministry, then, is not a matter of choice; but an ordinance of Christ. If any use the term "a hireling ministry" as a reproach, that reproach falls, not upon the labourer, who is worthy of his hire, but on his Lord, who hath ordained that he shall live of that hire.

The QUALIFICATIONS of a pastor are in *graces* and *gifts*—graces that he may be a "faithful," gifts that he may be a "wise steward." No extent of learning, no force of intellect, no ecclesiastical authority, can qualify a man to "feed the Church of God." His primary qualification comes from the Holy Spirit, and without His grace he cannot, by any assemblage of gifts or preparations, be "thoroughly furnished" for his work. The apostles were taught and were commissioned by the Lord himself, yet even they were not permitted to go forth on the work of preaching his atonement, till they had been "endued with power from on high." He forbade them so to do, and commanded them to "tarry;" then ascending, sat above the world he had just bought, looking down, and seeing it lying in the wicked one, seeing its sons die, while the men who held in their hands the commission for its regeneration were inactive; yet he had enjoined that inaction, and for days and nights he looked upon our sinful world, and by his own authority withheld all effort for its conversion! Was not this intended as a most solemn lesson to the church in all ages, that on no ground whatever, no matter how momentous, no matter how urgent, was she to send a man to preach the Gospel, whose fitness consisted only in instructions and credentials? Was it not to teach her that for ever, and at all hazards, she must commit that work to those alone, who had waited before the throne of our ascended Redeemer, till they received the baptism of the Holy Ghost?

But grace, though absolutely essential to constitute a true pastor, is not the sole qualification. "Who is that *faithful* and *wise* steward whom his Lord shall make ruler over his household, to give them their portion of meat in due season?" (Luke xii.

42.) If he be not *faithful* he will not, and if he be not *wise* he cannot, give them their portion in due season. Fitly to administer the food of souls, requires, that he, who is to be charged with that office, shall, not be presumed, but proved to have received from God the wisdom and the utterance whereby he shall be made "apt to teach." Otherwise, he may stand all his life before an ill-taught and ill-warned people, feebly handling the verities of salvation, dealing forth Divine knowledge with an impotence that would not be tolerated in any other sphere, and rebuking the church for her hasty mission of him, by showing himself a workman that needeth to be ashamed.

The DUTIES of a pastor are to *instruct* and *govern* his flock. He must "feed the flock of God," must "preach the word, be instant in season and out of season, reprove, rebuke, exhort with all long-suffering and doctrine;" must "take heed to himself and to the doctrine, for, in doing this, he will save both himself and them that hear him." His charge, however, is not limited to teaching; he must "feed the flock, taking the *oversight* thereof." But in exercising this oversight he may not rule as a "lord over God's heritage;" but is called to watch for the souls of his people as one that must give account. The design for which he receives authority is not to give him eminence or power; but simply to place over the household one who will give them their portion of meat in due season, one who will distribute the food essential to health, and preserve the order essential to happiness. His eminence is a trust of unbounded responsibility, in the meek discharge of which he wins a glorious reward; but in perverting it to purposes of arrogance or tyranny will expose himself to fearful retribution (Luke xii. 45).

III. The ORDINANCES OF THE CHURCH are stated in the commission given by our Lord, "Go and teach all nations, baptizing them in the name of the Father, and of the Son, and of the Holy Ghost." Here we have the *word* and the *sacraments*, which constitute the great ordinances of the church throughout all ages. The sacraments require the assembling together of the members of the church, that they may, in fellowship, show forth the Lord's death till he come. The word requires the assembling together, not only of the Church, but of all who will hear; for the gospel is to be preached to every creature. Hence arises the great ordinance of public worship. We certainly are not at liberty to exclude all but true believers from the assembly where God's word is preached, with an idea of thereby becoming separate from the world. To deny any man, who is willing to hear words whereby he may be saved, the opportunity of doing so, is to assume a prerogative of fearful extent, and of no scriptural authority. One great design of every public assembly of God's people should be, that, " if one come in that believeth not," he may have the "secrets of his heart revealed," be judged, be condemned, and so constrained to " fall down on his face and worship God." The fear that the unbelieving should, by being admitted to the assembly of believers, be led to imagine themselves the children of God, does not warrant us in excluding them when we are totally without scriptural precedent for such a step. And, moreover, the danger of the ungodly lies, not so much in imagining that they are saints; as that their natural condition is one of light guilt and slender danger. The way to show them all its stains and all its dread, is, to bring them as much as possible under that word whose entrance giveth light. Then as to the opinion that we should not call upon them to join in prayer or praise, because it is asking them to do that for which they have no ability; the same principle would forbid our calling upon them to repent and to believe, and would have hindered the Divine Being from saying, "Look unto me, and be ye saved, all the ends of the earth." It is our duty to call upon men to repent, to believe, to worship, and fall down, and kneel before the Lord our Maker. We have no power to give them that grace by which alone they can do any of these acceptably, and we have no right to withhold the call of Him who can accompany that call with power.

IV. The MISSION OF THE CHURCH is to "teach all nations, baptizing them in the name of the Father, and of the Son, and of the Holy Ghost." This mission is plainly not alone to *inform* all nations of the gospel; but to subdue them to it, and to its ever-blessed Triune Author, " baptizing them" into his name. The church is God's instrument for communicating himself to sinful men. Collectively, she says, " Come!" but every one " that heareth" is also bound with his individual voice to say, " Come!" The church exists only in her members. There is no abstraction by which holiness is preserved, though all hearts be worldly; and usefulness effected, though all hands be idle. You, my brethren, who love God, who know the Redeemer's grace, you are the salt of the earth. This mission of such glorious import is in your hand. You are as much bound to make Christ known as to know him, to preach him to others as to believe on him yourself, to commend his grace to those who know not its sweetness, as to draw for your own soul a daily supply.

Upon this mission the church does not journey alone. The Lord set it before her just as he was about to pass from her sight, and she was in danger of thinking, when she saw him disappear, that the task was heavy, and that he had left her to work it alone. But, just on the point of departing, he said, " I am with you;" she saw him rise, she looked at her work, "I am with you" sounded in her ear, and she could not feel alone. He filleth all things, he never forgets a promise, and his word " I am with you" seals upon the heart of his church the full certainty that her work is helped by his own right hand. That work is commanded to continue, and that glorious presence promised to crown it, " always, even unto the end of the world."

Questions of the church largely occupy many Christians. Yet one cannot study those questions in the New Testament without being struck that it is so full of the Saviour, and contains so little of the church. Not one epistle is written, not one discourse recorded, which had for its object the exposition of ecclesiastical polity. The Apostles fully argue and minutely apply every point of Christian doctrine, Christian experience, and Christian practise; but how rarely and how briefly do they touch upon the constitution of the church! And our glorified Lord, looking down upon the seven churches, writes to rebuke five, and to encourage two; but yet does not glance at a single point of mere economy. The only matters of discipline which receive from him any notice, are just the points we have set forth,—the duty of cutting off evil doctrines and evil doers.

Oh that Christians were more zealous for the Saviour, and less zealous for the church! How could I satisfy myself that I was pleasing my Master by persuading his children that, in order to join me and mine, they must forsake the communion of those, by whose hands he sought them, with whom he found them, with whom he carried them in his arms during their infant feebleness, and with whom he was edifying and blessing them up to the hour when I came to summon them to a controversy on questions of the church? No, I can far more certainly feel that I please my Master, by feeling that all these are one with me, because they are one with him; and by encouraging them to spread a sweet savour of Christ in their circle, rather than by importuning them to increase my own. Where they find the true Gospel, where they find the Saviour, I dare not intrude. If Christ be there, I should be bold to require that his members should depart, and that, above all, on the ground of " coming out of the world." The world does not preach Christ crucified, the world does not awaken dead souls, the world does not lead inquirers to the Lamb of God, the world does not shed upon believers the sanctifying influence of the Lord's presence. On what ground dare I tell those who are where they have found all this, that they are in the world? I dare not do so. I dare not imply that, to find Christ's Church, they must join my community, which, by such an assumption, would be cut off from the universal unity of the Lord's body, and erected into a separate and sapless limb. Above all, I dare not tell my Lord, that he is in the world, being found himself where none of his people ought to be found.

Brethren in the love of Jesus, pant not for uniformity; the search has always produced division, the attainment, so far as attained, death. This uniformity is nowhere described in the New Testament, and nowhere enjoined. Seek it not. Hail all your Father's children, as sweetly one with you. Do not allow any partition to abridge your joy, in a full sense of that holy oneness. Feel it closer than brotherhood; enjoy it; openly avow it; lovingly manifest it; and your own soul will have far more peace, your Lord far more honour, and the world a far more potent testimony to the Gospel, than if you ponder the errors of your brethren, till you judge it a duty to live apart.

W. A.

Printed by Libri Plureos GmbH in Hamburg, Germany